Computer Wizards

Word Magic

Claire Pye and Paul Virr

W
FRANKLIN WATTS
LONDON•SYDNEY

First published in 2003 by:
Franklin Watts
96 Leonard Street
London EC2A 4XD

Franklin Watts Australia
45-51 Huntley Street
Alexandria
NSW 2015

Created by:
act-two
346 Old Street
London EC1V 9RB
www.act-two.com

Text: Paul Virr
Consultant: John Siraj-Blatchford
Managing editor: Claire Pye
Editor: Deborah Kespert
Designers: Ariadne Boyle, Tim Clear
Illustrators: Ian Cunliffe, Andrew Peters
Art director: Belinda Webster
Editorial director: Jane Wilsher

A CIP catalogue record for this book
is available from the British Library.

ISBN 0 7496 4855 4

Printed in Hong Kong, China

Microsoft® Windows® and Microsoft® Word are
registered trademarks of Microsoft Corporation
in the United States and/or other countries.
Screenshots reproduced with the permission
of Microsoft Corporation.

Contents

Words marked in **bold** in the text are explained on page 32.

How to use this book
Look at the pictures in this book to find out what's happening on your computer screen.

Follow each numbered step in the book and on your computer.

1 Double-click on Microsoft Word.

Coloured arrows show you where to look on your computer screen.

Words that are underlined tell you what to do next.

Your tools

This book is about a **computer program** called Microsoft Word. It's like an amazing typewriter that helps you make words big and small and even different colours!

Big screen
This is your computer screen. When you type words, they appear here.

Cool keys
You'll need to do lots of typing in this book! You type using your keyboard.

Space
To make a space between each word, hit the Space bar.

My Poem

A **big** blue elephant
Had a small orange hat.

"*Miaow!*" squawked the hat,
"I'm not a hat. I'm a cat!"

"Bless my bananas!" **boomed** the elephant,
"A talking <u>hat</u>? Fancy that!"
"*A talking hat? Fancy that!*"

4

Mouse magic

When you move your mouse, a shape, called a **cursor**, moves around the screen. In this book, you'll need to move your cursor and click with your mouse. Here are the different ways of clicking.

Perfect poem

In this book, you'll find out how to type a poem and turn it into a work of art!

Click
Press the left button on your mouse, once.

Backspace

To delete a letter you've just typed, press the Backspace key.

Double-click
Press the left button twice, quickly.

Enter key

To start typing on a new line, press the Enter key.

Right-click
Press the right mouse button, once.

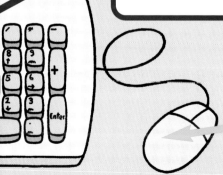

Mouse

Your mouse isn't a pet. You use it to point at things on the screen!

5

Getting started

Are you ready to begin? Let's open
Microsoft Word and start writing a poem!

1 Can you see
Microsoft Word on your
computer? <u>Double-click
on it with your mouse.</u>

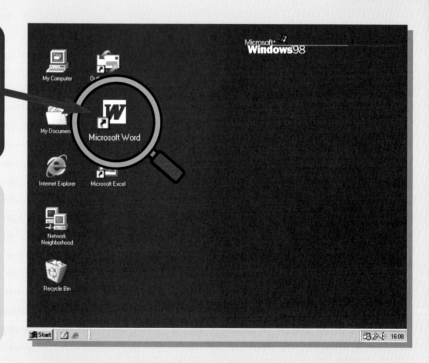

2 The white page on
your computer screen
is like a blank page in
a notebook. This is
where you start typing.

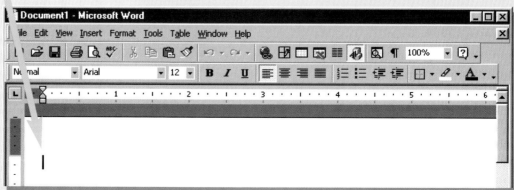

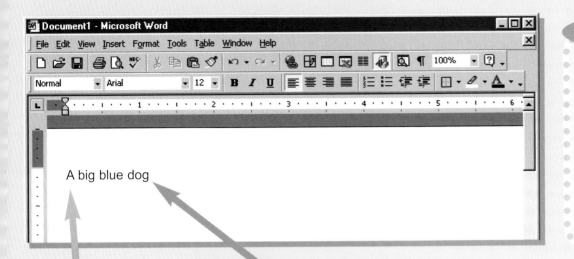

A big blue dog

Hey presto!

Capital letters trick

To type a capital letter, such as **A**, press the Shift key  and the letter **'A'** at the same time. Try typing these capital letters: **B C D.**

3 Use your keyboard to type these words on to your page.

4 If you make a mistake, it's easy to correct it! Let's **delete** the word 'dog'. Find the Backspace key [←] on your keyboard and press it three times.

5 Now type the word 'elephant'.

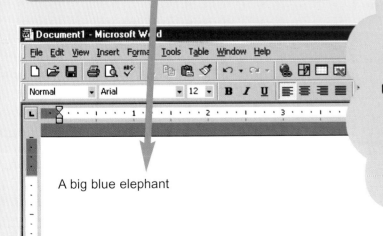

A big blue elephant

You've turned a dog into an elephant! Now try more animal magic by typing and deleting other animal names.

7

Save your work

Save your work and give it a name,
so you can come back and find it later!

1 If you switch your computer off before you save your work, it will be gone forever! Find this Save button and click it.

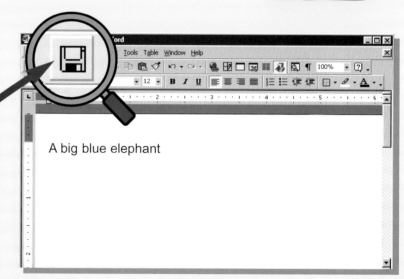

A big blue elephant

2 There's a special **folder** for storing all your work. It's called My Documents. Click the My Documents button to make sure you save your work in the right folder.

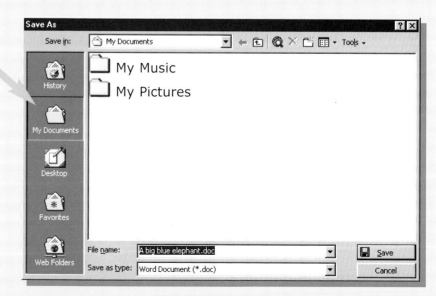

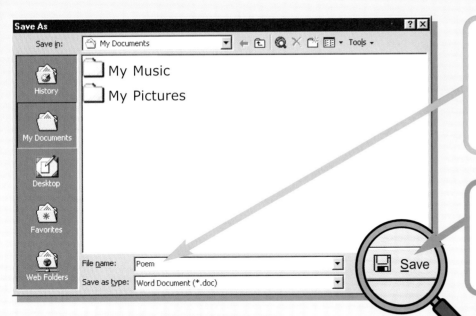

3 Type a name for your **document**. We've typed the name 'Poem'.

4 Now find this Save button and click on it.

Saving your work is important! When you make new changes, always remember to save them by clicking on the Save button.

Poem.doc - Microsoft Word

File Edit ~~View~~ Insert Format Tools Table Window

Normal Arial 12 **B** *I*

A big blue elephant

5 You can see the name you've given your document up here.

Start a new line

Put more words into place
on a new line of your poem.

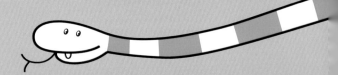

1 This flashing line is
a **cursor**. It shows where
your words will appear
when you type them.
<u>Press the Enter key
on your keyboard.</u>

2 The cursor jumps
to the next line, ready
for you to start typing!

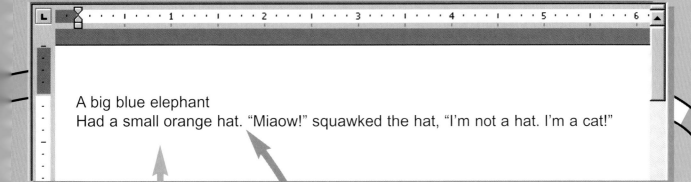

A big blue elephant
Had a small orange hat. "Miaow!" squawked the hat, "I'm not a hat. I'm a cat!"

3 Can you type all these words into your poem?

4 You can turn a long line like this into two shorter lines. To do that, click your mouse between 'hat' and 'Miaow'. Then press your Enter key.

5 To make an extra space between lines, press Enter again.

6 Finally, make a line after 'hat', here. Abracadabra, you've made a poem!

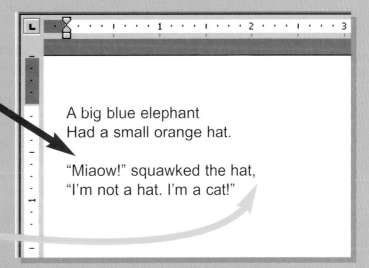

A big blue elephant
Had a small orange hat.

"Miaow!" squawked the hat,
"I'm not a hat. I'm a cat!"

Cut, copy and paste

Let's find out how to cut, copy and paste,
without any scissors or glue!

Look at our poem.
We've added two
more lines! Now copy
the same words into
your poem.

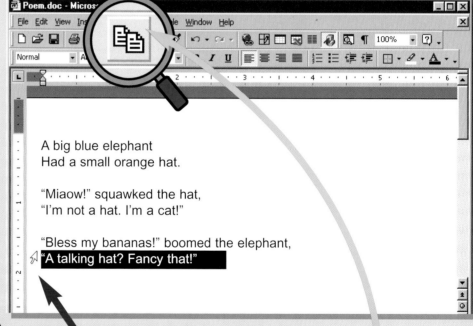

Poem.doc - Micros...

File Edit View In... ... le Window Help

Normal

A big blue elephant
Had a small orange hat.

"Miaow!" squawked the hat,
"I'm not a hat. I'm a cat!"

"Bless my bananas!" boomed the elephant,
"A talking hat? Fancy that!"

1 Point your **cursor**
at the beginning of the
line. It changes into a
white arrow. <u>Click with
your mouse to **select**
the whole line.</u>

2 Find this Copy
<u>button and click on it.</u>

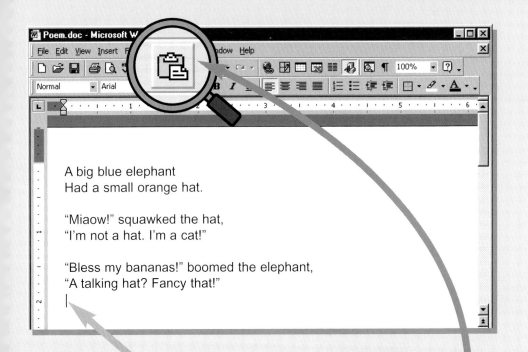

Hey presto!

Cut it out!
Make lines disappear, then appear again in a different place! Select a line, then click the Cut button ✂ to cut it out. Now click in another place. Find the Paste button 📋 and click it. Hey presto, your line has moved!

3 Choose where to put the line. Point your cursor at the end of your poem and press Enter.

4 Find the Paste button and click on it.

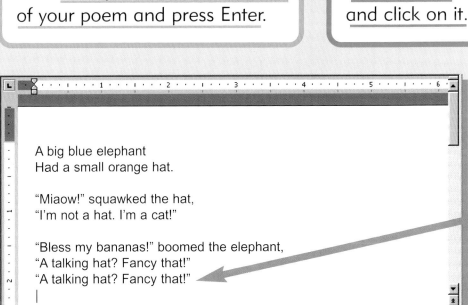

5 Ta-da! As if by magic, your line appears! Why not try more magic copying and pasting?

Bold, italic, underline

Here are a few tricks to make the
words of your poem really stand out!

1 Try this neat way to **select**
one word. <u>Point your **cursor** at
the word 'big' and double-click.</u>

2 Now find this Bold
button and click on it.

3 Has anything happened?
<u>Click anywhere in your poem
to see a change.</u>

Poem.doc - Microsoft Word

File Edit View Insert Format Tools Ta... Help

Normal   Arial

A big blue elephant
Had a small orange hat.

"Miaow!" squawked the hat,
"I'm not a hat. I'm a cat!"

"Bless my bananas!" boomed the elephant,
"A talking hat? Fancy that!"
"A talking hat? Fancy that!"

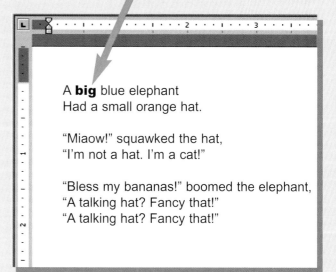

A **big** blue elephant
Had a small orange hat.

"Miaow!" squawked the hat,
"I'm not a hat. I'm a cat!"

"Bless my bananas!" boomed the elephant,
"A talking hat? Fancy that!"
"A talking hat? Fancy that!"

4 Now select the word 'Miaow' with a double-click.

5 This time, find the Italic button and click on it.

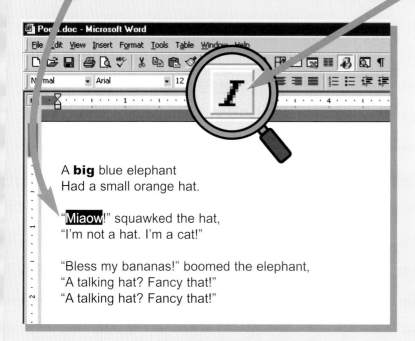

6 Click anywhere in your poem to see the transformation!

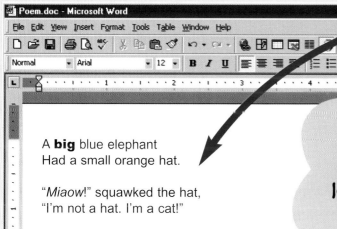

Copy the other words we have made bold and italic. Then, look in the Hey presto! box and try some magic underlining!

15

Words big and small

Here's a spell that you should know,
to make your words shrink or grow!

1 Let's make the word 'big' really big! <u>Double-click on the word to **select** it.</u>

2 Now find this **Font** Size box and click on the arrow next to it.

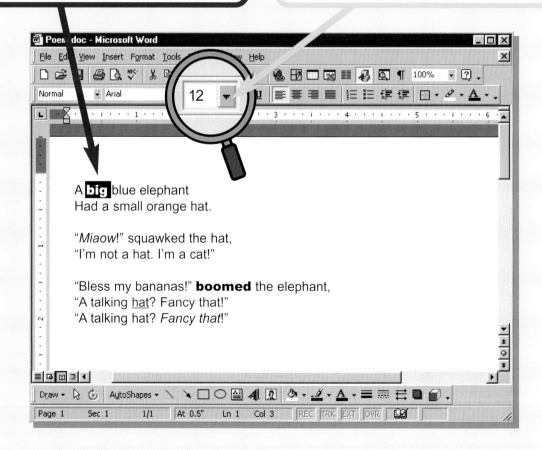

3 Choose a new size for your word. We've chosen a huge size! Click on the number 26.

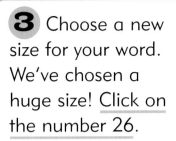

4 Click anywhere in your poem to see how big the word has grown.

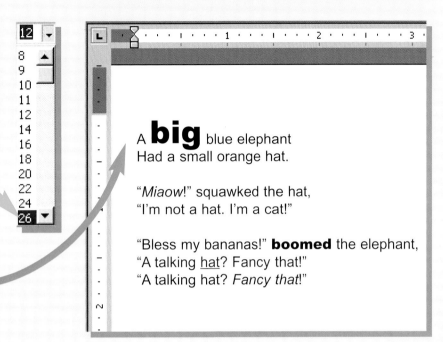

A **big** blue elephant
Had a small orange hat.

"*Miaow*!" squawked the hat,
"I'm not a hat. I'm a cat!"

"Bless my bananas!" **boomed** the elephant,
"A talking <u>hat</u>? Fancy that!"
"A talking hat? *Fancy that*!"

5 Now make the word 'small' really small. Select the word. Then click the arrow and click the number eight.

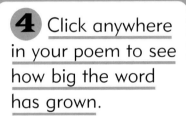

6 Click anywhere in your poem. Can you see how your word has shrunk to a really small size?

A **big** blue elephant
Had a small orange hat.

"*Miaow*!" squawked the hat,
"I'm not a hat. I'm a cat!"

"Bless my bananas!" **boomed** the elephant,
"A talking <u>hat</u>? Fancy that!"
"A talking hat? *Fancy that*!"

Letter styles

Different people have different handwriting,
so why not change the style of your letters?

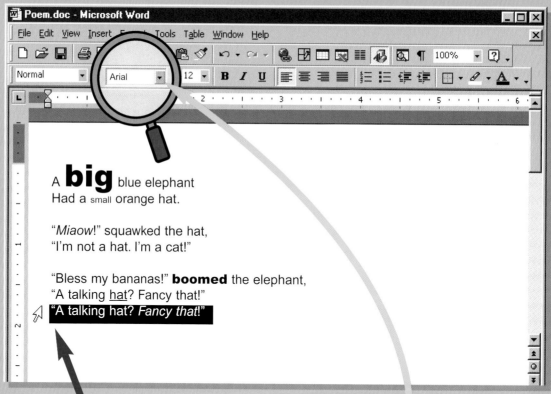

1 First, move your **cursor** to the beginning of the last line of the poem. Click once to **select** the whole line.

2 Now find this **Font** box. Click on the arrow button next to it.

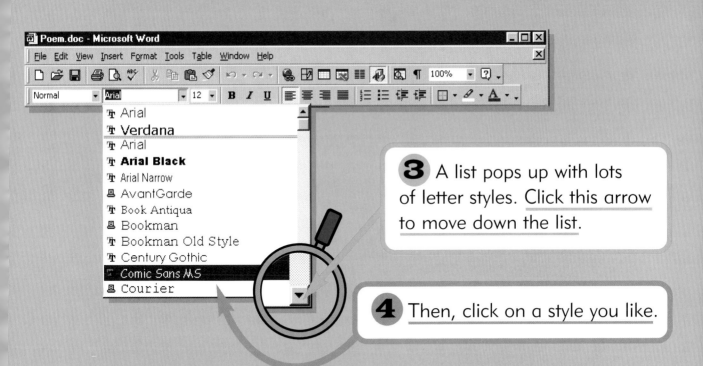

3 A list pops up with lots of letter styles. <u>Click this arrow to move down the list.</u>

4 <u>Then, click on a style you like.</u>

5 <u>Click anywhere in your poem to see the results!</u>

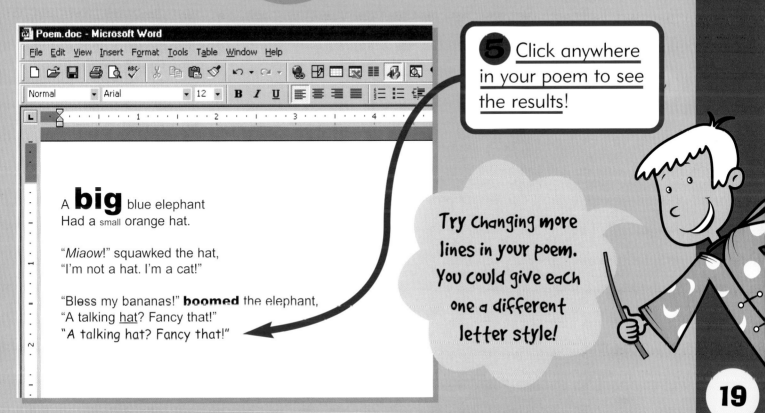

A **big** blue elephant
Had a small orange hat.

"*Miaow!*" squawked the hat,
"I'm not a hat. I'm a cat!"

"Bless my bananas!" **boomed** the elephant,
"A talking <u>hat</u>? Fancy that!"
"A talking hat? Fancy that!"

Try changing more lines in your poem. You could give each one a different letter style!

Splash of colour

Make the words in your poem
different colours. It's colour magic!

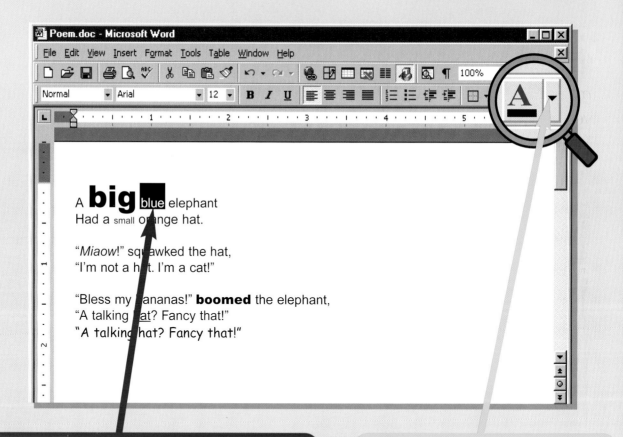

A **big** blue elephant
Had a small orange hat.

"*Miaow*!" squawked the hat,
"I'm not a hat. I'm a cat!"

"Bless my bananas!" **boomed** the elephant,
"A talking cat? Fancy that!"
"*A talking hat? Fancy that!*"

1 First, choose a word in your poem. We've chosen the word 'blue'. Double-click on the word to **select** it.

2 Find this **Font** Colour button. Click on the arrow next to the button.

3 A box, just like a paint box, appears. Click on the colour blue to make the word blue.

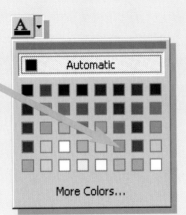

Automatic

More Colors...

Hey presto!

Invisible writing trick
To write a secret message, change the colour of the words to white. Then click your mouse and they vanish! To read your message, change the colour to black again.

4 Now click your mouse anywhere in your poem. Your word has turned blue!

Are you a clever copycat? I've changed the colour of a few more words. Can you do the same to your poem?

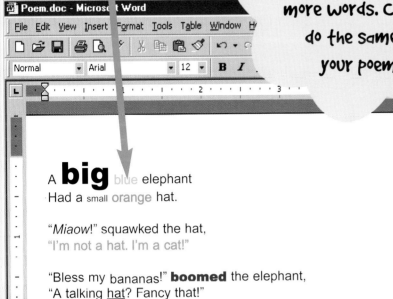

Poem.doc - Microsoft Word

File Edit View Insert Format Tools Table Window H

Normal   Arial   12   **B** *I*

A **big** blue elephant
Had a small orange hat.

"*Miaow*!" squawked the hat,
"I'm not a hat. I'm a cat!"

"Bless my bananas!" **boomed** the elephant,
"A talking hat? Fancy that!"
"A talking hat? Fancy that!"

Line up your words

Make the words of your poem
line up just how you want them!

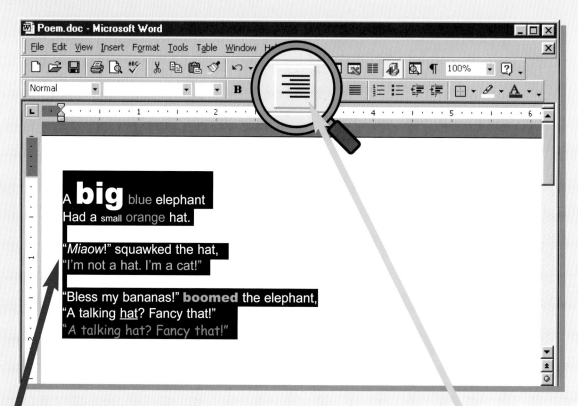

1 First **select** the whole poem. Press the Control key `Ctrl` on your keyboard and the letter 'A' at the same time.

2 At the moment, your poem is neatly lined up on the left side of the page. Find this Align Right button and click on it.

3 Hey presto! Your poem is lined up on the right!

4 Now find the Centre button and click on it.

A **big** blue elephant
Had a small orange hat.

"*Miaow!*" squawked the hat,
"I'm not a hat. I'm a cat!"

"Bless my bananas!" **boomed** the elephant,
"A talking <u>hat</u>? Fancy that!"
"*A talking hat? Fancy that!*"

5 Click anywhere in the poem to see your change!

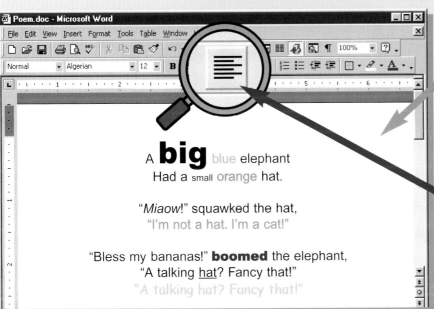

A **big** blue elephant
Had a small orange hat.

"*Miaow!*" squawked the hat,
"I'm not a hat. I'm a cat!"

"Bless my bananas!" **boomed** the elephant,
"A talking <u>hat</u>? Fancy that!"
"*A talking hat? Fancy that!*"

6 If you want to line up your poem on the left again, use the Align Left button. Which way do you like it best?

fancy titles

Put the finishing touch to your poem by giving it a fancy title!

1 First, make space for your poem's title. Put your **cursor** at the start of your poem and press Enter three times.

2 Click on this WordArt button.

3 Click on a WordArt style.

A **big** blue elephant
Had a small orange hat.

"*Miaow*!" squawked the hat,
"I'm not a hat. I'm a cat!"

"Bless my bananas!" **boomed** the elephant,
"A talking <u>hat</u>? Fancy that!"
"*A talking hat? Fancy that!*"

4 Click OK.

5 Type in the title of your poem.

6 Now click on the OK button.

7 Has your title jumped into the middle of the page? Don't worry! Move it into place using the arrow keys on your keyboard.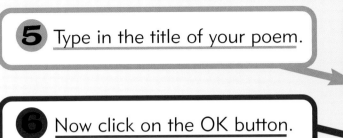

A **big** blue elephant

"M... My Poem at,
"I'm not a hat. I'm a cat!"

"Bless my bananas!" **boomed** the elephant,
"A talking <u>hat</u>? Fancy that!"
"A talking hat? Fancy that!"

8 Click anywhere on the page to see your finished poem and stylish title!

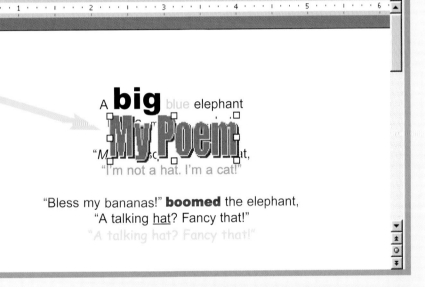

A **big** blue elephant
Had a small orange hat.

"*Miaow*!" squawked the hat,
"I'm not a hat. I'm a cat!"

"Bless my bananas!" **boomed** the elephant,
"A talking <u>hat</u>? Fancy that!"
"A talking hat? Fancy that!"

Printing time!

That's it! Now you can print out your poem.
It's a work of art, ready for the wall!

1 First, click on this Print Preview button to see
how great your poem will look when it's printed.

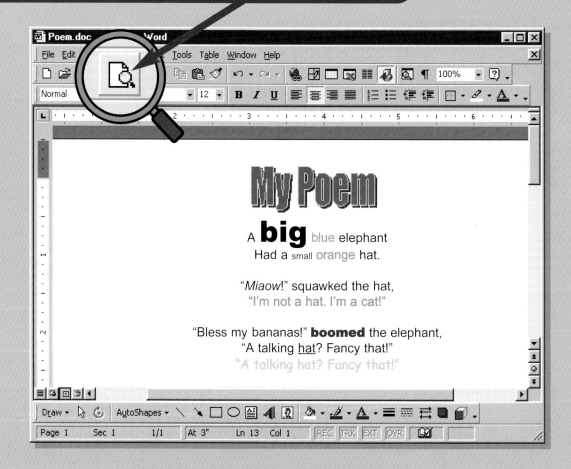

2 Wow, this poem looks really wizard! It's time to click the Print button to print it out.

3 It's simple to go back to your poem to do more work. Just click on this Close button.

Poem.doc (Preview) - Microsoft Word

File   Edit   View   Insert   Format   Tools   Table   Window   Help

34%   Close

My Poem

A **big** blue elephant
Had a small orange hat.

"*Miaow*!" squawked the hat,
"I'm not a hat. I'm a cat!"

"Bless my bananas!" **boomed** the elephant,
"A talking hat? Fancy that!"
"A talking hat? Fancy that!"

Page 1   Sec 1

Why don't you print out your new poem for a friend? You could even send it to your school magazine!

Find your work

It's time to close Word and then track down your poem again.

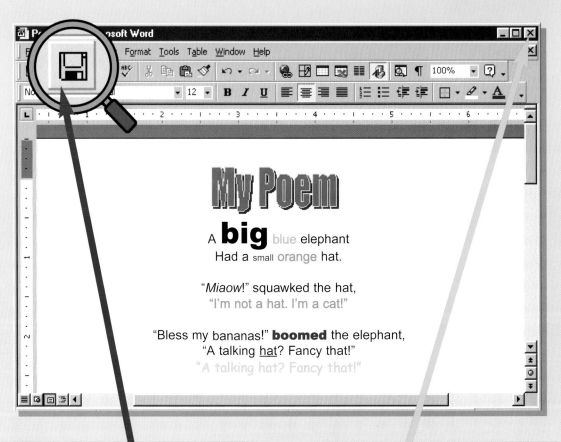

1 When you stop working, remember to save! <u>Find the Save button and click on it</u>.

2 Now close Word. <u>Click on the Close button in the top right-hand corner</u>.

3 To open your poem again, start by finding it! It's saved in the My Documents folder. Double-click on the folder to open it.

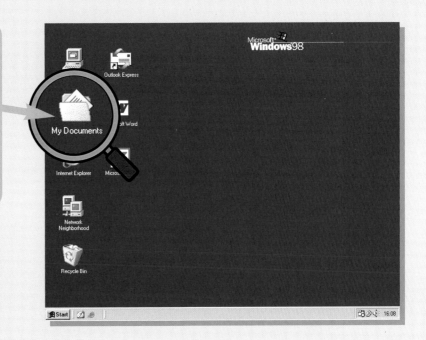

4 Now double-click on your poem to make it appear.

Wow! You really are a Word wizard. Why not try out your computer magic to make more great documents?

Guidance notes

This book aims to show children how they can have fun and be creative with words using a word processing program called Microsoft Word.

Microsoft Word

Microsoft Word is part of the Microsoft Office suite of programs. You can use this book with Office '97, 2000 and XP, although there may be slight variations in buttons and toolbars.

Macintosh users

This book is compatible with Microsoft Word Macintosh Edition. Please note that mouse clicks work differently with Macintosh computers and some buttons and toolbars may look different.

How to set up your computer

Children will find it easier to follow the steps if you set up your computer to look like the one in the book. Here's how.

Your desktop

Create a Word shortcut on the desktop.
1 Click Start, open Programs and find Word.
2 Right-click on the Word shortcut and drag it to a blank space on your desktop.
3 Select 'Create shortcut here' from the menu.

Word toolbars

Now open Microsoft Word and make sure the following toolbars are showing.
1 Right-click on a blank area of the grey toolbars at the top of Word.
2 Make sure that only the following toolbars are ticked: Standard, Formatting, Drawing.

Word font

We've made Arial the default font for our lessons because it is easy for children to read. To change the default font to Arial:
1 Open the Format menu and click Font.
2 Select Arial, Regular and 12 from the menus.
3 Click the Default button.
4 Click Yes.
5 Click OK.

Print Layout view

Print Layout view is a clear way for children to view their work. Here's how to set it up.
1 Click on View, then select Print Layout.

Extension activities

Each chapter of Word Magic is self-contained so children can learn at their own pace. Hey presto! boxes contain tips and ideas for extra practice. There are more extension activities on the following page.

Typing and deleting

Encourage children to develop typing skills by exploring their keyboard and correcting mistakes with the Backspace key. Show them how to double-click on a word to select it and then delete it with the Backspace key.

Save your work

Children should save their work often! It's good practice to save work in My Documents so it's easy to find later. However, if children are working on a network, you may need to set up individually named folders and show them how to find them in the Save As dialog box.

Be creative

Using Word to transform text is magic! Children can make posters, poems, cards and labels. Why not type a paragraph of text children have been reading in class, and transform it for display?

For a group project, children can type different paragraphs from a text, style them and then paste together the full text for display.

Make it fun!

Ask children about what they are doing and invite them to think about what they are going to do next. Encourage and praise them as they learn, and remember not to cover too much at once!

Health and safety

Supervise children when turning the computer on and off. Remind them not to put their fingers inside the computer at any time. Encourage them to take regular breaks to avoid repetitive strain injuries and eyestrain. Refer to the computer manual for information about the correct seating and posture. Children should be sitting upright with their feet on the floor and the keyboard in line with their elbows.

National Curriculum links for Information and Communication Technology

Key stage 1

Finding things out
- ✔ 1b. Entering and storing information in a variety of forms.
- ✔ 1c. Retrieving information that has been stored.

Developing ideas
- ✔ 2d. Trying things out and exploring what happens in real and imaginary situations.

Exchanging and sharing information
- ✔ 3a. Sharing ideas by presenting information in a variety of forms.
- ✔ 3b. Presenting completed work effectively.

Key stage 2

Developing ideas and making things happen
- ✔ 2a. Developing and refining ideas by bringing together, organising and reorganising text, tables, images and sound as appropriate.

Reviewing, modifying and evaluating work
- ✔ 4b. Pupils should describe and talk about the effectiveness of their work with ICT, comparing it with other methods and considering the effect it has on others.

Scottish National Guidelines 5-14 ICT

Strands covered at levels A and B
- ✔ Using the technology
- ✔ Creating and presenting

Useful words

computer program

A computer program helps you to do different jobs on your computer. In this book, we use a program called Microsoft Word to create a colourful poem.

cursor

The cursor is what moves on screen when you move your mouse. You use it to point to different parts of your screen.

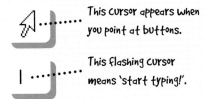

This cursor appears when you point at buttons.

This flashing cursor means 'start typing!'.

delete

Delete means erase or rub out. In this book, you use the Backspace key to delete letters and words from your document.

document

A piece of work you create in Word is called a document. Poems, stories and letters are all documents.

folder

A computer folder is used for storing work, just like a real folder. In this book, you store your poem in a folder called My Documents.

My Documents

font

A font is the letter style you choose for your words. This font list shows a few of the different fonts you can use in Word.

select

Select is another word for 'choose'. In this book, you point at a word and double-click on it to select it. The word you have selected is highlighted in black.

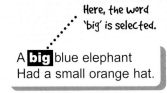

Here, the word 'big' is selected.

A **big** blue elephant
Had a small orange hat.

Index